لـ/ه/ل

At the Seashore

First published in the United States
in 1991 by Gallery Books, an imprint of
W.H. Smith Publishers, Inc.,
New York, New York 10016.

First published in Great Britain
by Kingfisher Books Ltd.

Gallery Books are available for bulk purchase
for sales promotions and premium use. For
details write or telephone the Manager of
Special Sales, W.H. Smith Publishers, Inc.,
112 Madison Avenue, New York, New York 10016.
(212) 532–6600.

ISBN 0-8317-7356-1
Printed in Spain

READY SET GO

At the Seashore

Penny Lloyd

Illustrated by Katy Sleight

GALLERY BOOKS
An Imprint of W. H. Smith Publishers Inc.
112 Madison Avenue
New York City 10016

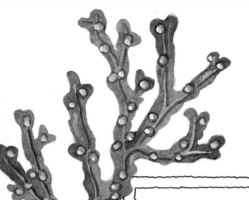

Contents

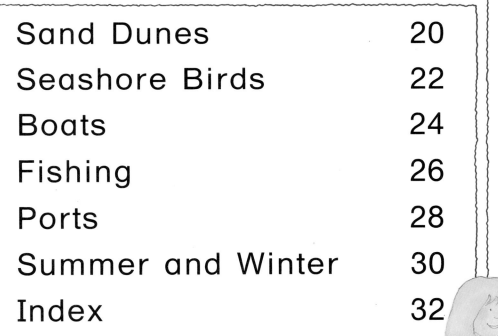

Welcome to the Beach

Can you find these things in the picture?

6

Sand

Sand is fine.

Sand is crunchy.

Sand is dry.

Sand is wet.

Can you build a sandcastle?

Sand is soft.

Sand has shells in it.

Sand hides worms.

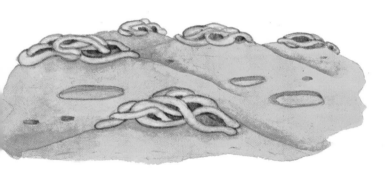

Sand is many
different colors.

Waves

Waves are good to splash in . . .

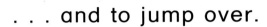

. . . and to jump over.

They wash away sandcastles . . .

. . . and tickle your toes.

Waves break on many different shores.

Waves can crash . . .

. . . or gently ripple.

They carry animals . . .

. . . and toss boats at sea.

Where have you seen waves?

11

The Tideline

The tide comes in twice a day and the sea covers most of the sand. When the tide goes out again the waves leave treasures behind.

Some of the things left behind by the tide.

Cuttlefish bone

Seaweed

Barnacles

Shells

Driftwood

Can you make a treasure chest?

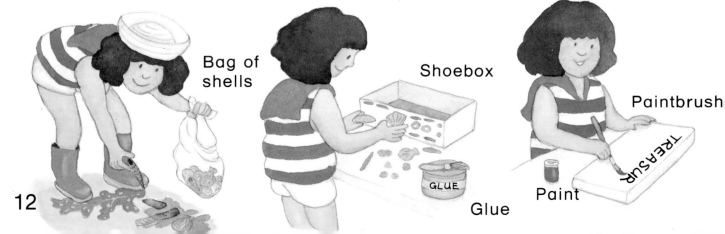

Bag of shells

Shoebox

Paintbrush

GLUE

Paint

Glue

TREASUR

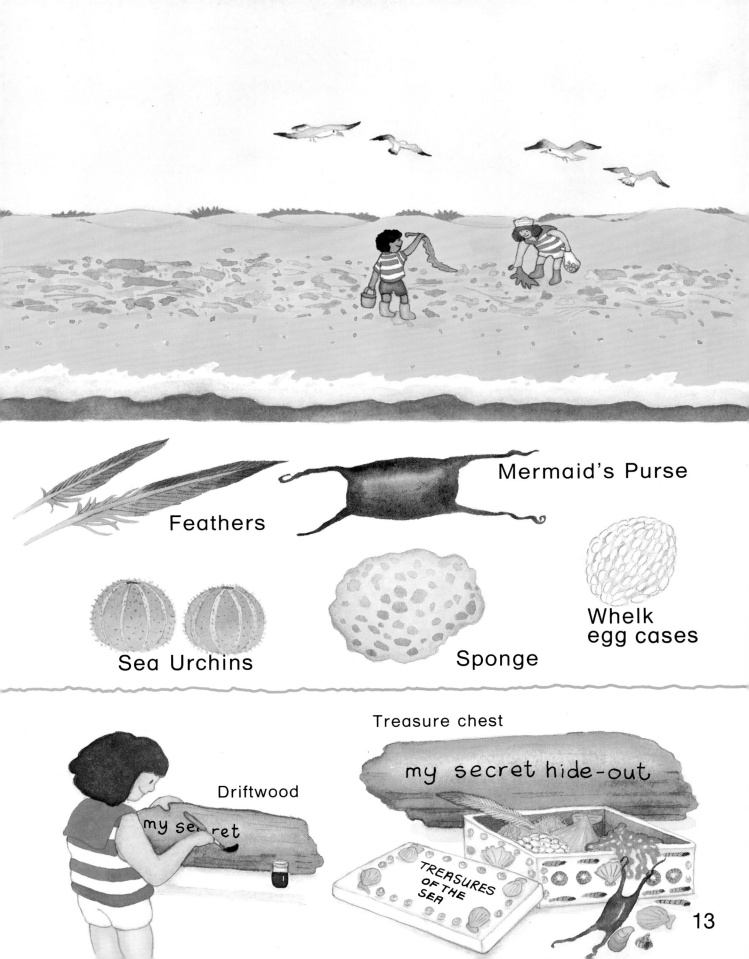

Mermaid's Purse

Feathers

Sea Urchins

Sponge

Whelk
egg cases

Treasure chest

my secret hide-out

Driftwood

my secret

TREASURES
OF THE
SEA

13

Rock Pools

When the tide goes out,
the sea leaves pools of
water among the rocks.

Can you find these animals in the rock pool?

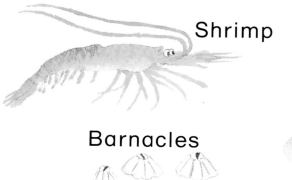

Shrimp

Barnacles

Sea Squirts

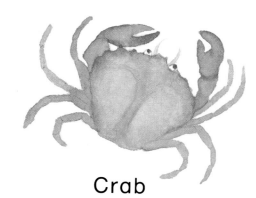

Crab

Hermit Crab

Anemones

Starfish

Fish

Limpets

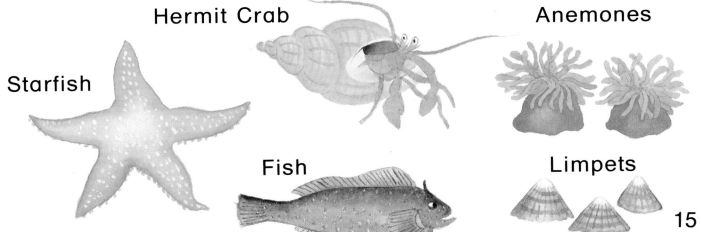

Seashells

Many animals which live in the sea have shells.

Sometimes the tide leaves empty shells on the beach.

Cockle

Razor Shell

Tower Shell

Cowrie

16

Can you find these animals in the sea?

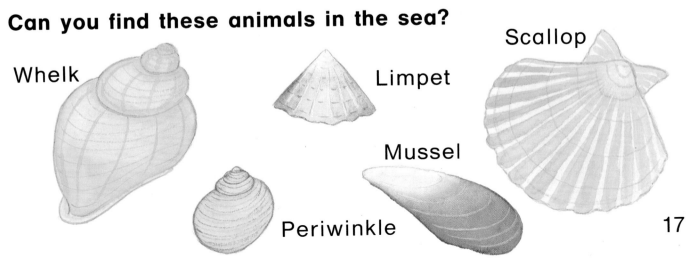

Whelk

Limpet

Scallop

Mussel

Periwinkle

17

Seaweed

Seaweed grows on rocks. Sometimes rough waves wrench it off the rocks and leave it on the beach.

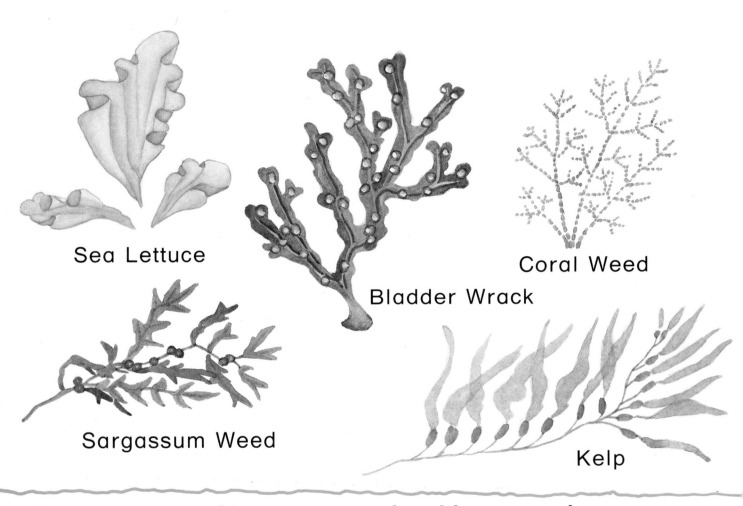

Sea Lettuce

Bladder Wrack

Coral Weed

Sargassum Weed

Kelp

Here are some things you can do with seaweed.

Pretending to be . . .

a mermaid

a pirate

Neptune

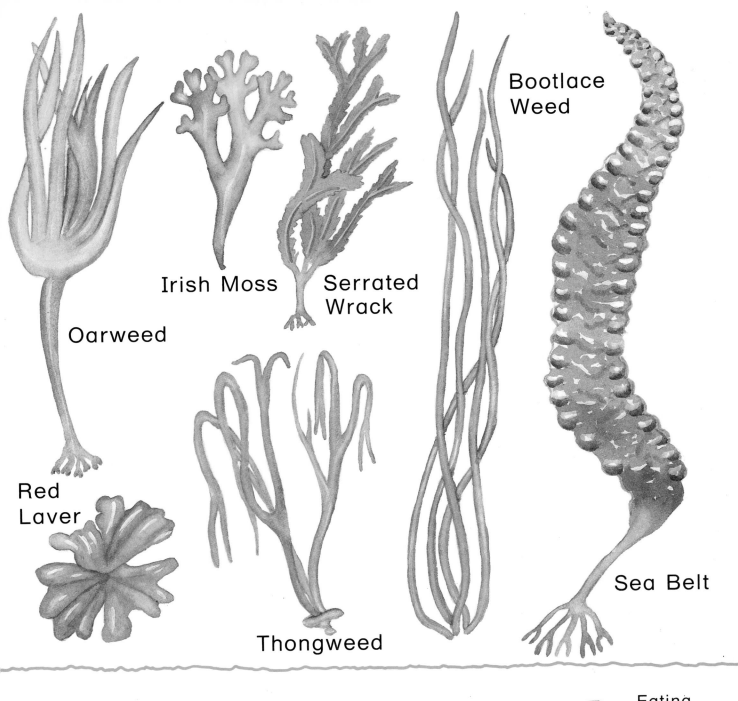

Oarweed

Irish Moss

Serrated Wrack

Bootlace Weed

Red Laver

Thongweed

Sea Belt

Making a picture

Eating laver bread

Eating seaweed with rice balls

Sand Dunes

On the edge of some beaches are hills of sand, called sand dunes. Sand dunes are covered in plants which help keep the sand in place. Many animals live on the dunes. How many can you see in this picture?

Can you find these flowers and grasses?

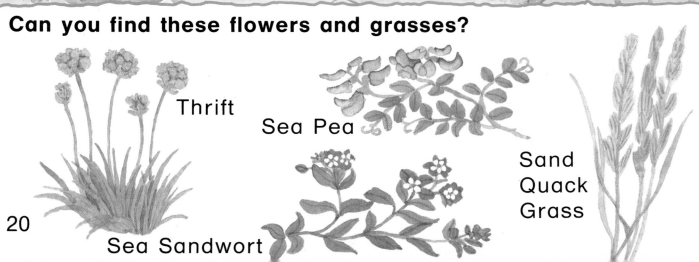

Thrift

Sea Pea

Sea Sandwort

Sand Quack Grass

20

PROTECTED AREA

DO NOT WALK ON
THE SAND DUNES.
USE THE WALKWAY
PROVIDED.

Sea Holly

Gorse

Sea
Bindweed

Marram
Grass

Seashore Birds

Gannets dive.

Plovers paddle.

Terns swoop.

Oyster catchers wade.

Puffins swim under the water.

Which birds are we pretending to be?

Soaring

Gliding

Diving

Swooping

Seagulls
wheel and soar.

Falcons hover.

Dunlins
circle and glide.

Cormorants
stretch out
their wings.

Sandpipers
skim the water.

Sanderlings
scurry along the seashore.

Stretching

Scurrying

Paddling

Wading

23

Boats

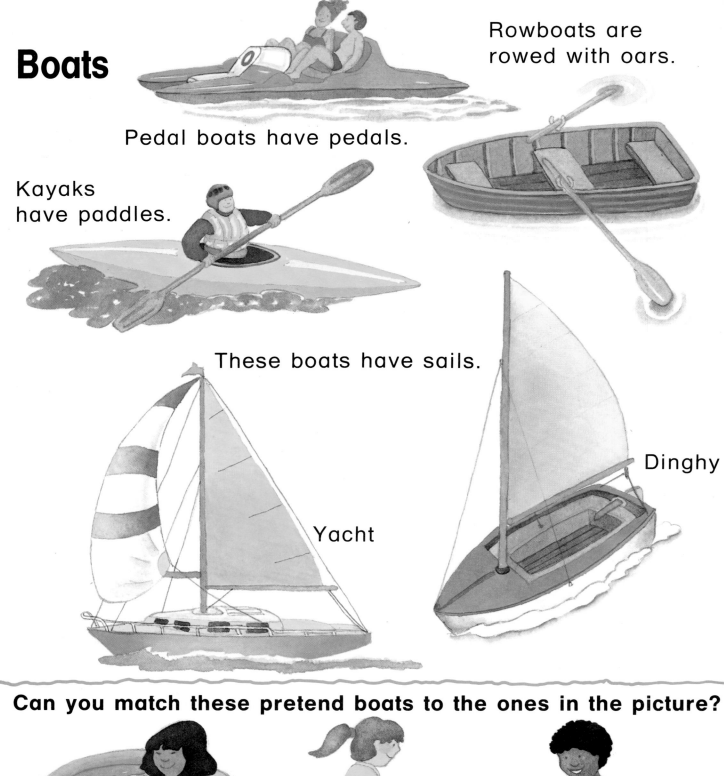

Pedal boats have pedals.

Rowboats are rowed with oars.

Kayaks have paddles.

These boats have sails.

Yacht

Dinghy

Can you match these pretend boats to the ones in the picture?

These boats are powered by engines.

Speedboat

Motor cruiser

Lifeboat

Ocean liner

man overboard!

Fishing

Fishermen bring their trawlers and fishing boats into the harbor at the end of the fishing trip. They unload their catch at the quayside. Some of the fish is bought at once. The rest is packed in ice, loaded onto trucks and taken to the fishmarkets.

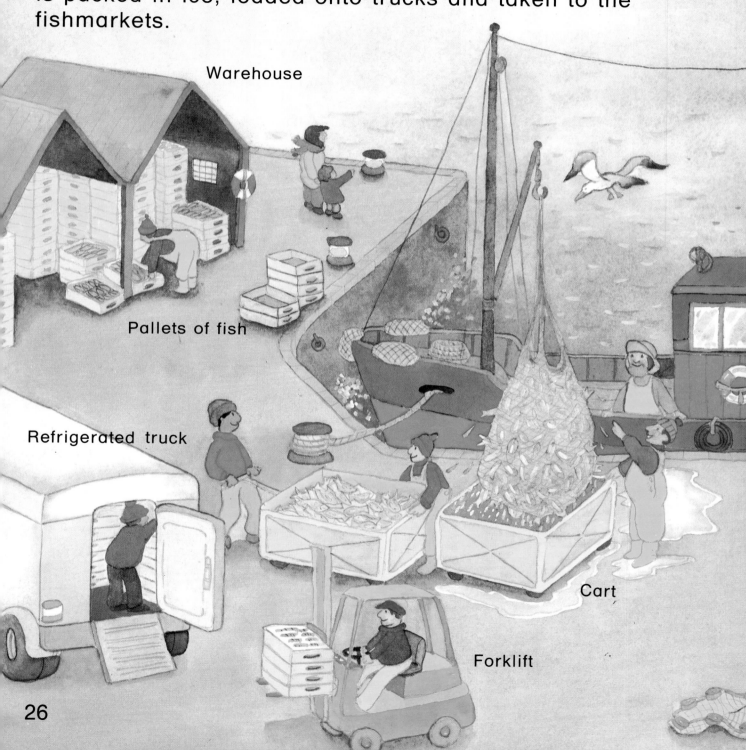

Warehouse

Pallets of fish

Refrigerated truck

Cart

Forklift

Fishing rods

Lobster pots

Motorboat

Trawler

Fish stall

Mending nets

27

Ports

At the port, cargo ships are loaded and unloaded and people board cruise liners, ferries, and hovercraft to travel by sea.

Passenger ferry

Foot passengers

Crane

PORT STATION

Cargo ship

Hovercraft

RESTAURANT

Cars

Camper

29

Summer

Here is the seaside in summer and in winter.

30

Winter

Can you see the changes?

How many fish can you find on the coral reef?

Index

You can find all these seaside plants and animals on the pages listed below.

If you look closely at the picture above you will find an emperor angelfish, a scorpion fish, a butterfly fish, a parrot fish, a lyre tail wrasse, a yellow-tailed blue damsel fish, tomato clown fish, a banded pipefish, a cardinal fish, and a surgeon fish.